This Poem Might Save You *(Me)*

This Poem Might Save You *(Me)*

Jesenia Chávez

Copyright © 2022

All rights reserved. No part of this publication may be reproduced, distributed without the prior written permission of the publisher, except in the case of brief quotations embodied in critical reviews and certain other noncommercial uses permitted by copyright law. For permission requests, write to the publisher, addressed "attention: Permissions Coordinator," at the e-mail address below.

davina@alegriamagazine.com

Library of Congress Control number: 2022905374

ISBN: 978-1-7379927-9-0

Published by Alegria Publishing
Book cover and layout by Carlos Mendoza

"To survive the Borderlands you must live sin fronteras be a crossroads."

-Gloria Anzaldúa

A Poem Can Be A Time capsule

A poem can be a time capsule
Capturing a moment of distress
A memory to revisit,
a moment to share and release,
to share and relive

CONTENTS

Preface	13
Mangos	15
Listening	17
La tormenta	18
98 casi 100	20
What is it about the mornings?	22
La Feria	23
At the end of the day	24
Dos coyotes	25
To the boys who broke my heart and are now men	26
Gracias Selena	28
Thoughts While on the Freeway	29
Grief	30
At the hour	31
Uprooted Roots	32
IF.FOUND.	34
Home Keys	35
Maybe This Time	36
Separated	37
The thing about Mexico	38
My confidence has grown	40
La maestra	41
Girls WAKE solitas #WEBEENWOKE	42
Gracias manos y manitas	44
Bachatéame baby	45
The baby and the dog	46
Hybrid Católica y Apostólica	48
Dicen	49
Oleada	50
Warrior womyn	51
When you watch someone die	52
Mi abuelita era pura magia	54
This is the price we pay	56
This poem might save you *(me)*	58
The thing about sisters	60
Careless man	62

Untitled haiku #7	63
41 Lessons from 41 years on Planeta Tierra	64
Airport blues	66
Pink Suitcase	67
Prayer for the pain	68
una hija	69
It's Getting Hot in here/ So Hot in Here	70
Hospital Vending Machines	72
Inspired	73
Dando vueltas	74
Clean bathroom	76
When the journal pages are complete	77
Las movies	78
Sunday Service	80
Clown mask	82
The company I keep	83
Planned parenthood protestors	84
15 Month Pandemic Home Transformed	85
Can I?	86
11:50am highland park, CAlifaztlan, October 31, 2021	87
Tu Eres mi Tesoro	88
Sisters	90
The falcon knows more	91
Translation	92
Group Text	94
Glass Window Facts!	96
Baby Yoda, is that you Grandma?	98
Christmas day	100
Baby Mario	102
Wilted	104
Tree	104
I forget you	105
I am not a mom and why do you care?	106
Tears for Fears: The Poem, Not the Band	107
Ode to my Ears	108
Schools are magical spaces	110
Weekly Screen Time Report, Who Asked You, Bro?	112
El Arroyo	114
Aknowledgments	117
Bio	119

Preface

As a Chicanita from a big Mexican family, I found great joy in reading and retreating into the pages of books. I remember my sisters and I walking to the tiny Maywood Library (now called the Maywood Cesar Chavez Library) in Southeast Los Angeles and checking books out. But the truth is that I had never seen myself, my family, or my experiences reflected in text until a mentor in high school gave me a copy of Sandra Cisneros's House on Mango Street.

Reading that book became a defining moment for me. For the first time, I finally felt seen and validated. Cisneros's stories echoed through my mind and planted a seed of hope. I nurtured that seed in college by writing and reading books and poetry by women of color. I devoured every book I could get my hands on and often read for pleasure rather than the required reading for my courses. (Don't worry, I still graduated.)

This seed had not been allowed to bloom because my insecurities and fears stopped me from pursuing a career in the arts. My immigrant parents didn't work for me to be a struggling artist, I thought. So, I put that dream to rest and continued writing, posting, sharing, and reading at open mic events when I could. Years later, I attended an event at the Museum of Latin American Art in Long Beach to hear Sandra Cisneros speak. She shared her thoughts about the need for more women of color to write and be published. She did not want her book to be the only one that little brown girls everywhere could read. Cisneros encouraged us to create, write, and tell our stories. She inspired me. She watered the seed, but I was not ready.

When the pandemic began, I took up crocheting and gardening like most people. I then realized that there is no time like the present to make our dreams come true. To nurture those parts of ourselves that do not want to die, that do not want to shrivel up into hard rocks of bitterness. I realized que si no ahora, entonces cuándo? The only person in my way was me. These poems were born out of a desire to share my stories and the words that keep me up at night. The words that burst out of me, accompany me on walks, and come to me through the voices of my beloved familia. They come as whispers, as shouts, and from the words that were never uttered by my departed loved ones. These words come from all the women's voices who must stay silent to survive. They come from the little girl who dreams of seeing her name and words on the spine of a book in the library.

The beauty is in the process, in the grays, the in-between that children of immigrants feel. The taste of English and Spanish on the tongue. Of hot dogs, tortillas, and weenie con huevo, too.
These poems are an offering from my soul to yours, and I thank you for supporting a dream. I hope you are inspired, annoyed, amused, and most of all, I hope that you nurture your dreams. Through my collection, This Poem Might Save You (Me), I invite you to take a journey with me.

Mangos

En Dolores, Chihuahua crecen muchos mangos, the weather is humid and it rains in the evenings and all the mosquitos bite your arms and legs, and they hover around the lights.
Their buzzing sound making a blood sucking symphony, the lights lead them to their doom.
But some get away and suck on our sweaty bodies,
Those mangos are a treat and there's nothing like that first bite, after traveling along a bouncy dirt road, con el cuerpo sacudido,
It leaves a sticky face and sticky hands after feasting on mango after mango, sitting on the porch of my abuelita's house
the juice drips down onto your thighs as you sit on the plastic white chairs, pile after pile of peels and the huesos,
the red bucket is always full, the ripest ones attract the flies, but who cares we sit on the porch y platicamos, y cómo estás, y qué has hecho, y por qué no tienes novio ni marido muchacha
pero nadie me pregunta de mis otros logros, porque aquí no hay otra salida que con marido
we eat the mangos, we peel them, the flesh gets stuck in our teeth, and that doesn't stop us, y nadie te critica, well at least not to your face

the juice drips onto the dirt floor my great aunt works so hard at keeping clean and this confused me when I was a kid because I didn't understand why she was cleaning dirt, I mean its dirt right?
Mom yells at me, "no comas muchos mangos porque te va dar chorro"
Later in the outhouse those words haunt me as I crouch down on the hole in the ground, flashlight in hand, praying there's no alacranes
But we don't listen, these mangos are home, these mangos don't need chile or limon solo así solitos se disfruta mejor.
When the mango bucket gets dangerously low, we go and get some more, the fallen ones,
the ones you can grab on your tippy toes, and the rest with the stick with the wire on the end, and if you feel brave, you climb the tree in your chanclas to throw them down and "accidentally" hit las primas on the head for a little mango revenge
My little Tía Licha was my favorite mango eater, she was a little person and she was old, and she was fun to look at because as a kid I thought she was magical because I had seen the movie Willow and was mesmerized at my

Tía Licha eating mangos
She would eat, she had some missing teeth so it was more difficult for her, and I would stare. She would eat and wipe her hands on her apron that she never took off, only to sleep and go to church.
She enjoyed her mangos and talked with a mouthful of flesh in her mouth and I loved her for this abandonment, the sheer joy of eating mango.
Mango here is not the same, it doesn't taste like home,
But once in a while the sweet scent, the peels piled up from the fruta man, the hairs on the hueso of the mango transport me for one second, to home to the spirits of people that were once on that porch with me eating those mangos, but are now en el cielo comiendo con los angelitos who are probably still wondering why I don't got a man, and I bet the mangos there are just **heavenly.**

Listening

I hear the birds and the hammers and the fireworks and the shots, the chants of black lives matter and defund the police and "hey hey ho ho racist police have got to go"
And no justice no peace, no justice no peace
I hear sirens and loud alarms on everyone's homes announcing the lockdowns,
I hear the voices, the voices, saying there's another world possible and we are listening, mostly
We are listening

I am listening to my heart, it beats and beats, I hear my blood pulsing through my veins, my body is excited, long before my mind, my body hopes for peace and healing, my mind is catching up, I hear Breonna Taylor, I hear her mom cry and I hear the cries for not one more, no more kids in cages, no more murders
I hear the youth shouting, they say no more, they say no more, they say no more.
We've been waiting, tearing down the monuments to the nation's racist past, I hear concrete crumbling, the foundation being torn out, I feel my feet shake, I feel the quake, this is the big one we've been waiting for, the big one to knock down the walls of hatred and fear, knock it down, burn it to the ground
We will rise, we will rise together
No justice no peace, no justice no peace we chant it together, all the colors, all the love, I hear it, I hold on to it, I yearn for it like a long lost lover, I am ready for it, I am listening, breathing, I can breathe, the pollution from the factories hasn't killed me yet, I CAN breathe, I CAN hope, I can speak, I WILL listen.

La tormenta

When the storm started Tía Licha, mom, Stephanie, Tía Delfina, Tía Pancha, and I ran indoors
we crowded into the two small rooms laughing,
and Tía Licha began to pray as she lit some candles,
the smell of wet earth and burning wax filled the room,
the sounds of the hail pelting the tin roof,
the swell of rain seemingly out of nowhere,
the storm its own life,
its own sound,
stopping in its own time.
we sat around on the beds and waited for the storm to pass,
it was only a few minutes, and the worse was over,
soon we would go outside and see the damage,
Tía Licha murmured prayers.

I wish I would have paid more attention,
I wish I could remember every word, but I only remember whispers and laughs,

   during the storm we prayed and relighted those stubbed out wicks,
      before the storm we pray
      after the storm we pray
     for Tía Delfina to recognize us,
     for her blank stare to turn into warmth
for her old self to come out and sweep and say some harsh remarks lovingly,
      her pañuelo on her head,
      her apron always on,
     like all the señoras of the house.

This Poem Might Save You *(Me)*

We prayed for no more deaths,
we prayed for tíos and tías and primos to be safe,
some were, but others were killed,
the guns too readily available turning a trivial argument deadly.

Now, we pray for their souls in heaven,
or more likely they pray for our souls on earth,
the dead reminding me,
the storm waking us to see and laugh and fear nature,
the storm it came and hit me on the head to see the moment,
to get in my body and connect,
los muertos me visitan y me recuerdan, hay que rezar mija, rezar,
recuerdame,
no olvides la tormenta.

98 casi 100

Mi abuelita iba cumplir 98 años el 31 de julio. Pero ya no está con nosotros y a todas nos duele mucho.
Como te llegas acostumbrar a que una luz en tu vida se extingue
Everything is barren without her life force
It's a giant space in your heart that is tender and sad
She was always a fixture in our lives
She was always there
Since I was born, nursing me back to health because I was a fussy baby that didn't like formula and my mother's milk had dried out
She was always there to baby sit and make up words like "saralailo" for my brother Robert
She was always there in her apron, her apron where we'd stick our hands in for change for the paletero
She was always there with a pot of frijoles and her delicious salsa en el molcajete made with tomates and chiles from the backyard
A plate of frijoles and queso fresco and salsa, sitting with grandma and tía Panchita, what a slice of heaven
Her flowers being tended to, the roses, the beautiful roses
Did I appreciate it?
Did I know that we would lose my aunt to cancer and my grandma four years later?
Do we know how to appreciate people when they are here, en vivo, para hablar y abrazar y alimentar?

This Poem Might Save You *(Me)*

Do we know how special those prayers are, watching that rosario on TV every day, how silly I thought it was, still makes me chuckle if I'm being honest
Sitting on the porch in Maywood,
Eating an elote contigo abuelita y tía.
Maybe a raspado too if we felt rich
Little Elias hanging around, playing with me
One time I walked to the liquor to buy the meat for the chuletas Tía was gonna make for dinner, I felt so useful, can't cook, but I can walk to the carnicería at least
Watching univisión, horrified by Primer Impacto
Fans all on because it's so hot
Those moments en la sala, en el porch
How I miss them.
How an excerpt from a book, a smell, a funny meme about grandmas can instantly touch the ache and make it bleed out in tears
How we move on with our lives feels like a tragedy too, feels wrong somehow
But I know it is right, it is life and death and the in between
People we love will leave us, sometimes against their will
But it's still beautiful to love them
Buried in the same cemetery, en el calvario, mother and daughter, tía y abuela
para visitar y recorder y llorar, y cantar
para aplacar a los chamacos 'cuz they wanna play tag and leave already
The pain, it never goes away, but we find solace in the memories and the love
I remember we all stood around your bed as you took your last breaths and we prayed
We were with you on your trip out of this life, you held me in my earliest days, and I sat there on your last day
how everything is connected, how it never feels like enough time with the people you lost
Abuelita no cumplirás 98
Pero yo se que tengo tu presencia espiritual en mi vida, que te amo, y que nunca me faltará un bonito recuerdo de ti.
Maybe in heaven there's free Wifi y todo es traducido
So you and tía can read my Spanglish poem
Hechamé un like parientes, desde arriba lo recibo.

What is it about the mornings?

All seems possible in the morning, all the things will get done, even if you're not quite sure what the "things" are
The to-do list starts
The sun has risen
The race begins
The race against the clock
24 hours
23, 22, 21, 20, 19
Oh shit I've been laying in bed for 14
Exercise, work, coffee?
Rushing off to nowhere
Cleaning, radio on all day,
Sage the house, tend to the plantitas
Worry you are killing them, wonder if someone does house visits?
Lunch with friends? The swapmeet, oh no 5 hours left in the day
Get a massage, pedicure, coffee?
Eat
Sleep some more
In the morning I make grand plans
Then lay back down
The meditation helps
Work in spurts
When the energy is high
Cleaning frenzy
4 hours of daylight left
What to do, what to see
When it's just yourself to keep you company
Move, leave, clean, sit, stare at the screen, have I got any "likes"
Dreading my own company
Stare at the screen

La Feria

the fair came to the neighborhood once again for the long weekends,
it used to spread out for several blocks, but it's been getting smaller every year,
soon it'll be one raite and the elotero.
used to look forward to it every year. see we didn't leave the hood that often in those days
walked around with my primas and my sister, coqueteando, even got a free ride from the young carnie, bone-thugs-n-harmony on the tilt a whirl, thought I was gonna spin into oblivion,
ride stops. that didn't happen,

smell the hotdogs wrapped in bacon, there's no tofu in these meat by-products loud music playing from the stage and I have my mandatory fantasy moment, where I'm onstage and dozens, yes dozens of southeast residents applaud me, dotingly looking on

POOF! it's over, we walk down the street for the fourth time,
it's getting late,
gotta walk back home, or soon our parents will embarrass us by looking all over for us and then screaming.
but I wanna get on the Ferris wheel one more time. see the city from up top catch a glimpse of downtown, the tops of heads, maybe I'll see someone I know and I'll scream their name at the top of my lungs.
head home with a slight headache and a grumble in my stomach from all the junk, man could we spread out 5 dollars.
go back home, get in bed, debate whether or not I should sneak out and walk around for just five more minutes 'cuz I just know something fantastic is gonna happen,

if only I could be there for a little longer some handsome, young man is gonna come rescue me from my sadness, my madness, but no…

fear or common-sense wins. I stay, I sleep.

in the morning it's all packed up transformers style.

but they'll be back again.

At the end of the day

At the end of the day, I have markers, stickers, tardy notes in my pocket
Coffee stains and faded knees from bending down and tying shoes
I have a pang in my stomach 'cuz I'm hungry, I gotta pee and can't decide which is more urgent

At the end of the day, I feel exhausted and worried

I wonder where my students are going
If they'll be safe, if they'll get to see their parents, if they can afford rent and the electricity bill, I worry if what I'm doing is enough

I'm overwhelmed by the opinions swirling around me about my job and what I do, when most of those people have never taught a day in their life. I am disheartened by the talk of guns and, no thanks, I don't need one

At the end of the day, I remember I am only human

What about living wages, affordable housing, access to quality healthcare? Positive relationships, it only takes one to change a child's life, to build resiliency,

Can I be the one?

I can sign petitions, and go to protests, and vote, and email my congress people, I can sing songs and dance and run and take care of me too, I can be the best I can be

teach reading and writing and math and science and how to get along, and let's take care of each other, and let's do the yoga slide and breath

at the end of the day I hope I am making a difference,

I hope I can get up and do it again the next day

Dos coyotes

Today I saw a butterfly
I saw a hummingbird
And then I saw two coyotes,
Fluffy tails, staring back,
I approached cautiously, and of course brought out my phone to post about it

I approached and they walked on, at a leisurely pace, they could care less about me
They walked on and I walked on
and I grabbed a rock just in case, though I've heard they scare easily,
I mean humans are more of a menace to them.

A guy approaches and he says don't worry about it, I glance at the rock in my hand and feel a little embarrassed, because I'm tough.
But we chat a little and when coyotes are out of sight, I run down the mountain
I run and I feel free
I love the solitude of the hike, the quiet, the stillness, the swaying trees, the dead branches and the calm I feel.

Sometimes I feel lonely when I start a hike
But, one day I looked down and saw the tracks, so many different kinds of tennis shoes,
all those feet on the trail, feet that walked and ran,
just like I am doing,
big shoes and small shoes,
and dog prints and bird feet,
suddenly I felt surrounded by all of them

I looked down and felt less lonely,
thousands of footprints
Like the poem about Jesus carrying you on the sand,

These are the moments I feel connected to everyone,
and even in my solitude I can feel loved and love everything, too

To the boys who broke my heart and are now men

Boys who didn't have a kind momma or a kind dad
Boys who were stunted by addiction and abuse
Boys whose pain I can see
In those beautiful brown eyes

Boys to men
But not the band
Boys to men

I want you to dedicate a song to me on Art Laboe
An oldie
Like I'm your puppet

And I'll dedicate you one back
Each night before you go to bed my baby, say a little prayer for me my baby and tell all the stars above
This is dedicated to one I love

This Poem Might Save You *(Me)*

To the ones I've loved

To the boys who broke my heart
I appreciate you
'Cuz sometimes I learned something about me
About the way I love
And I ran to my pillow
To my journal
To books
To my friends
To therapy

And I learned to recognize my patterns
And each time I picked myself up
Til it hurt less and less

Til I blocked your number AND I blocked you on Instagram

And I only creep on ya once in a while, just out of curiosity
Porque la verdad es que
Mejor ella que yo
Y al final de cuentas
te deseo lo mejor

Gracias Selena

Selena, la pocha, la Tejana, Mexicana-Americana,
cuando te moriste que tragedia, estaba en el carro con la mamá de Lucy de chicle/pegoste como me apodó su familia, y anunciaron en la radio que había muerto Selena.
Recuerdo que nos sentimos tristes, pero realmente yo no te conocía muy bien Selena. Pero luego "Encuentro Musical Latino 199 quién sabe? No se, pero me tocó pasear en la carcacha hecha de cartón con Lucy en el teatro de Bell High School, cuando le hicimos un tributo a Selena, cuando yo era una estrella y brillaba mi talento en el escenario de Bell High con sus sillas duras de madera, y yo canté "el Chico de apartamento 512" y baile tanto que sentía que mis caderas y pies se iban apartar de mi y seguir bailando, and I danced Bidi, Bidi bom, bom, and Selena, we lost a bright star, and Selena, "late at night when all the world is sleeping, I stay up and think of you", and your dark hair and dark eyes, and curves and I thank you because we don't have many, Mexican-American, Chicanas, limited Spanish speaking, but NOT limited Spanish singing, cantantes, bailadoras, y con mucho Estilo like you! your popularity, presence and película con J-lo, inspire me and make me cry, pero "no me queda mas, que aguantar bien my derrota, y brindarte felicidad". Gracias, thank you, 'cuz I see me when I hear you, my nieces see themselves, "se emocionan, ya no razonan" y tu voz siempre vivirá, You live beyond your body's death, you live in our hearts, and your beautiful Tejana face and name is on t-shirts, and earrings, and pins, and key chains, and lipsticks and even pinche culture vultures reppin' you, and with our holy Chicana trinity of La Virgen, La Frida, y Selena forever, we dance la tecno cumbia with a shiny bra and red lipstick, sin apologies, a big smile and big hair, and a big PRESENCE, no matter if you were Jehova, I mean so was Prince, right? You Selena, along with your controlling father and amor prohibido all so relate-able I want to dance and sing and cry con GUSTO, to remember to feel that I matter, and my people matter, and I'm brown and beautiful, and my sister's are too, for this I thank you, pero "Aaaaaaaay, como me DUELE".

Thoughts While on the Freeway

Driving home today on the 110 North, brake lights for miles
Downtown L.A. high rises towering over me heading home to my studio apartment

Then, on the radio they announce the guilty verdict and I have to cry and breathe
I have to make sure I don't blur my glasses too much

I've already fainted once on the freeway
Doesn't need to happen again

I hear the verdict
I cry for all the lives lost.

Los Angeles, they announce is getting the unaccompanied minors, children as young as three years old
The heartbreaking image of little kids in the convention center floods my thoughts

Today, April 20, 2021
almost the anniversary of the L.A. uprisings in 1992
Yet this time we get to tell a different story
I drive home exhausted from hybrid learning and zoom class
too hot and COLD
Embarrassed that I feel so tired
Seven little kids in person
The rest online, if they show up at all.
Hours of planning
Hours of smiles and greetings, trying to communicate with my eyes
Swallow a couple bits of salad
to drive home
to the verdict to the news
While my own feelings flood me
But I will not drown in them
I notice them and I allow them to pass through me
And I send out the love, the hope, and I make sure to keep some of that for me, too.

Grief

Grief strikes in that soft part
It hurts and the tears flow
and the face distorts
It gets mixed in with all the other losses
A recipe for sadness you did not want
It's got too much salt
But it's there
the tightness in your chest is released
you can say goodbye and hope the angels are best friends
hope there is a heaven for our lost loved ones
maybe they run into each other at the cemetery gates,
in heaven, they are gathered in a place with no pain
they can feel all the love
all the heartbreak, too, and receive our embrace.

At that hour

Sometimes I wake up at that hour
The hour that caused me fear
But now causes me to pause,
it's the sunrise of my thoughts. I'm in them,
it's the hour that I question my decisions
If the man I lay next to will betray me
If I'm better off alone
If I chose the wrong job, the wrong major,
if I'm living the wrong life
It's that hour of loneliness, all the questions come forward,
should I get up?
Should I change jobs,
my life, my choices,
I question everything
But then I see the sun has not risen
and I roll on my side and go back to sleep

Uprooted Roots

I often feel uprooted, but I'm unsure where I should be planted
I often wonder, where is my home?
 everyone says it's deep inside of you.
Pero a veces se me hace difícil ubicarme.
Is there a GPS, a cure at home depot's garden section to help?
I am rooted in my Mexican/ Chicana/ Los Angeles Mexican girl identity.
I am from South East Los Angeles.
I am a gaucho, I am a bruin, I am survivor, I am an educator, a poet and a chillona, too.
I am rooted, but I often feel uprooted.
Are my roots diseased? Do they need to be cut?
I want to be replanted in fertile soil that is my own,
my own space,
my own land.

These roots of displacement go way back, historical trauma deep inside,
a sense of loss deep inside,
leaving me feeling empty and lonely, too, sometimes.
The roots inside me, the roots inside me, the roots inside me,
they need medicine,
they need fertile soil to be planted in the ground
to be uplifted with enough sunshine and water, too.

This Poem Might Save You *(Me)*

Sometimes I feel the tug of oneness
I feel connected, at ease,
I can hold on to the words and the spaces in between to find them.
Roots inside of me,

Perhaps if I say it enough, I will believe what everyone says,
I will feel like I belong everywhere.
I will find pretty planters and be replanted as often as I'd like.
I will pull on the complex network of roots and draw strength and love and energy
like they did it,
like they survived much harsher times, our grandmothers, our mothers, our ancestors
I can feel the tug I can feel the push
Lift your head up girl, levanta tu cabeza, tú vales mucho,
TÚ También perteneces a este lugar robado,
a este lugar violado,
a este lugar usado, es TU lugar
Tómalo, me gritan, me susurran, y a veces si escucho.

> Take it they scream!
> they whisper
> and sometimes
> sometimes,
> I listen

IF. FOUND.

What happens to the lost pets? The signs stay up and I wonder if Chester was ever found, or Pinky, he needs his meds, you know.
Do the owners come back and take the signs off if the pets are found? Or do they leave them, thinking perhaps the wind or a hormonal mean teen tore it down from the utility pole. Do they forget about those of us that worry about their lost pets? I'd like to collect some data on this, how many pets are found, how many are lost forever, does the sign help? The font? The size?
Do people prank call? Do they steal your pet and then sell it back to you for cash? Gentrification brings more bougie pets and owners who can afford big rewards for precious Fluffy with the sad eyes and bowtie.
And don't chase the dog if you see her, she scares easily, approach cautiously, like you would a man on the ledge, don't jump, live. Life is precious.
The lost pets, are they lost forever, run over? Stolen? In the pound? I'd like to think they just went off for an adventure, to the desert, no more stray dogs in Los Angeles streets, in Mexico they're still roaming, and no one seems to be bothered by them too much, they walk around, tranquilos, free.
I'd like to put up a sign, with no tangible reward. I'm searching for empathy. Can we care about and uplift each other? Look past the hate and the fear and the otherness. Can we stop fighting for the crumbs and look up? Can we say I hear you and I see you and I'm sorry? I will work to create a better world with you, and it starts with me in my heart, reprogramming, reeducating in my mind without the torture, books, books and more books, those help extend a hand to learn about another's experience.
Looking for EMPATHY,

IF FOUND, approach with mucho corazón to extend a hand, mask on to salute from

six feet apart. IF FOUND, please call, and I promise I'll take down the sign when I find it so you won't worry about it too much, so you won't worry every time you see the sign on the electric pole. IF FOUND, hold on to it, hold it close and please share it. I know I will.

IF FOUND, we can build together, IF FOUND, we can stop the killing. IF FOUND, we can destroy the cages and the walls. IF FOUND, we can LIVE, too. IF FOUND, call a friend. IF FOUND, we can, we can, we can, we can, we can, we can HOPE, we can LIVE, we can, WE CAN, I hope.

Home Keys

As I type away, the clock ticks, the time goes by.
I thank my strict High School teacher for the typing skills I got now.
I can type without staring at the keyboard with my fingers on the home keys like she taught us Typing away to express the anguish and sorrow, to explain mostly to myself, the feelings, the exhaustion, the losses, the fears
The letters forming words as I shed some tears
The letters forming the shape of my grief
What a relief
Typing away the laments and filling the page with my joy too
The smiles and the breeze and the birds incessant chirping no matter my mood
The blooming flowers on my walks and the familiar hawk
The raspado man, con elotes and all the hot chips and the duritos, too,
he's making jokes with the kids, "quieres sin hielo, o con hielo"
the jokes are free, the raspado $2.50
he even convinces them to try fresa con chicle flavor
the baby boy can hardly hold the footlong raspado, you get your money's worth.
I walk around searching for a fruit stand, pero no hay
I settle for a raspado de leche flavor and an elote
What a relief a walk on the streets can be.
because even when you're blue, you can't help but see the hope around you
Making a mental note for later when you can sit and type this poemita,
when you've wiped away the paralysis and found the medicine on the keyboard,
on the home keys like the teacher taught us

Maybe This Time

They will stop
Won't shoot a brown boy so soon
There won't be no tears, or blood
There won't be stories anger or crying mothers or blaming your skin
Graduations, be
Your future, your path, your choice
Not the tragic news

Separated

Separated from
Your familia, your mommy
How do we end this?

The thing about Mexico

There's lots of contradictions and guilt

The brown kids in the streets, the blond ones, too

El color te marca, te limita y te atrapa

The help, the helped and the in between

The dread like rasta
In the eyes of America
Own the land
Clean the land
Drink the land
The camarón y los lobsters
Rojos del sol
Quemazón
Pesos y dólares
maletas empacadas con los bikinis del swapmeet
flaquitos, flaquitas
motos y carritos de golf
Niñitos y niñitas trabajando y otros disfrutando
Unos con hambre por gusto
Y otros por pobreza
La panza gruñe con hambre

–Mi mamá los hizo y se tardó mucho para hacerlo– dice el niño
Me pregunto si se refiere a él y sus hermanitos,
o a las pulseras,
pero creo que los dos se tardaron mucho en hacer,
uno se vende más caro
Porque todo se vende para sobrevivir
Y quieres postre?
Mar y sal y arena
ruidos raros de insectos exóticos
pájaros, mariposas y un cangrejo caminando en el pasto del hotel

Mientras que yo tengo el privilegio de viajar, pensar, escribir, contemplar el horizonte

Porque tengo amigas generosas y tarjetas de crédito que me permiten viajar
ser de los que se sientan en la arena a comprar

Pero en otra vida, yo sería la niña vendiendo aretes y artesanías en las calles también Por qué no escoges donde ni con quien naces

En el mar la vida es más sabrosa como dice la canción

Aunque aquí, algunos tratan a los perros mejor

My confidence has grown

One day she showed up

she was always there

singing me a song
to love, to play
to be

-*Tu si puedes*- me decía pero no la escuchaba

Estaba sorda a sus gritos
A sus consejos
A sus empujones suavecitos hacia mi libertad

No la escuchaba porque lo demás la atrapaba

Pero ella siempre estaba a mi lado

En el viento
En los pajaritos que cantan y las flores
Y las canciones de la radio
Siempre allí
Sin tener que hacer nada más que respirar y sonreír

La maestra

te quiere mucho
te compra libros y juguetitos
a veces llora contigo también y desea poder pagar tu renta
darte papeles
para que no vivas con ese miedo de la migra
para que tengas días llenos de alegría y diversión
desea que las rentas no fueran tan caras
que los trabajos pagaran mejor
que los hombres no golpearan a las mujeres y que tuvieras más ayuda
para que disfrutes de la infancia
sin tener que sufrir tanto
solo poquito, las cosas de la niñez
como si te caes de la bici, o se te pierde tu juguete favorito
espera que puedas respirar aire libre andar por las calles sin sentir temor por
los hombres tirados en el piso que diario pasas en camino a la escuela
la maestra te desea lo mejor
espera que entres a jugar y soñar
aunque sea por un ratito sonreír y platicar
porque la maestra siempre se sintió segura y protegida en la escuela
espera que puedas tu también
juntas creamos espacios llenos de magia y compasión
juntos bailamos y brincamos y nos peleamos
pero nos amamos siempre
porque duramos todo el día juntitos en el salón
y tus cuentos, historias, y dibujos viven en mi corazón

Girls WAKE solitas #WEBEENWOKE

We get up and go to school and make breakfast for the little ones, explore the possibilities and dodge perverts on the street
Girls wake themselves and go through the day with a sinking feeling,
but at least at school everything is predictable and if you're good everyone will treat you good too
We walk with our sisters, and books on tape,
and Nancy Drew books because those are your favorite

Ride bikes around the neighborhood and stare at cute boys,
they stop at the railroad tracks and throw a couple rocks around, reshuffling 'em for fun and head back home for a weenie on a fork you heat up on the stove.
Rescue kitty cats from the bushes in the front and take them home as pets
Dance and pretend to be in a band,
barbie and the rockets, play teacher and church
and she's the priest this time and go get some pan to be the ostia,
and play commercials, too, "it's Channel 9, live from Maywood"
you pretend to make out with teddy bears like they do in the novelas,
play with the bricks in the backyard for the wall your tío is building and then your cousin gets a bloody toe and pretends to be you at the clinic for the free healthcare,
the trail of blood leaving the evidence of playing cruise ship.
Sometimes we play bank and drive through
rehearsing at adulthood

This Poem Might Save You *(Me)*

girls wake themselves and play hide and seek and el señor de la noche
and tell dirty pepito jokes you don't really understand,
we go through every part of the house and backyard and garage, and even the roof,
and we are always searching for something,
some treasure, some secret
and sometimes you find 'em, but mostly you don't and one time you step all over the car in the garage and get in big trouble and cry 'cuz you get hit with the belt.
We play barbie and make a mess in the living room making a little casita and family for your barbies, and they're all single moms.
you hurry up and clean up the toys and wipe everything down and clean 'cuz it's almost 5pm and your mom and dad will be pissed if they see the mess.

We buy a big stick or a fudgesicle from the paletero depending on your mood
searching frantically for some change all around the house, or screw it
you break your alcancía and splurge. Search for your chanclas under the bed
or you run out descalza 'cuz your parents aren't home anyway.
Play with the best toy you got, the easy bake oven, and you make little cakes until the mix runs out, you eat 'em all up and get a stomach ache.

The best days are the ones after Christmas Eve 'cuz you pack up all your new toys and take 'em to your cousin's house 5 blocks away so you can play together for hours.
Your sisters, your cousins, your best friends,
your adventures and wandering all the more fun, 'cuz even though you wake yourself,
you're not alone, you got your posse, your squad, your confidants, your heart
you wake yourself 'cuz parents are busy at work, and you wonder if other kids have moms who wake them and comb their hair and make their breakfast,
but not us,
not these girls
they wake themselves
yesterday, today and always. Holding hands facing the world with a tribe of mujeres always behind you, and in front of you. AND beside you, too.

Gracias manos y manitas

old wrinkled soft hand,
hands that have washed many dishes
held me as a baby
held 'em in my substance induced breakdowns or drunkenness
sacred hands that have held the rosary hundreds of times
in prayer for everyone
even if they were lost for a little while and broke your heart
held masa de tamales
my hair as I puked
little baby hands that held finger for support as I took my first steps
hands that wrote a kind word
to strum the guitar and sing those old songs with the tías
held the wheel and got me home safe
a hand to keep me from falling
or to pick me up from the mess I made
to do my hair, en esas trenzas apretadas que me encantan
To feed me
zip me up
spray sunblock
brush hair away from my face to tickle
to tease
to lead
hands that dried my tears
And soothed my fears.
Hands down your hands have held me up.
I appreciate all the hands and the bodies they're attached to
I wanna hold your hand,
in closeness
in support,
to show you that I love you.
Dame la mano,
I PROMISE afterward I'll wash my hands.

Bachatéame baby

Shiny top and tight pants,
mid riffs, glittery salsa shoes
ombligos libres y sueltos foreheads touch,

hands and hips,
twirls and dips,
hair in your face, your own and sometimes others,
standing around and hustling for a dance,
"would you like to dance?"
a hand offered just when you were going to quit and sit down

or go to the bathroom

or the bar
or glance around to see if your friends are at least having more luck

that first dance is always a bit awkward and stiff,
but the vodka soda is now entering your bloodstream

helping you relax

sometimes you don't even need it
a few dances to warm up and get in the groove,
intimacy with strangers,
I feel like the ocean and the waves
gliding along to the music

The baby and the dog

When hiking,
the couples with the baby in the backpack and the dog annoy me the most

they remind me of the lack
the inadequacy I feel

like something is wrong with me
like I missed the meeting, the memo
the class about how to get married and buy a house and have a baby and a dog by 35 or younger or at least before 40

the clock has ticked away.

I missed the class about how to get the wedding.

the couples with the baby and the dog annoy me the most, and I want to snicker at them,
or at least shake my head in disgust.
Now I know how the wicked witch felt,

why she cursed the baby,
why she wanted to take Snow White's beauty, or the voice from little mermaid,

I want to be mean, too
but I don't because that's just rude
and when they get closer, the baby is kinda cute and the dog, too

and though my body has not swelled with growing life inside

and my left finger has not felt the weight of a diamond,

I have felt my body swell with joy and pride while dancing, traveling, reading, writing,

I have felt the weight of a silver ring I bought myself,
a heart to remind me,
I love me.
I free myself from the expectations others have placed on me

the expectations I placed on myself

I free myself

even though the couples with the baby and dog annoy me the most, I understand this is my path
I'd like to think I chose it,
I remind myself over and over,
breathing in and out, running fast now,
running fast to escape the couples with the babies and the dog toward my own wholeness.

Hybrid Católica y Apostólica

The symbols swirl
The altar you created for you
Con imágenes de la virgen
Un buddha y velas
Your religión, your healing space is you
Sage, incense, palo santo, una giant concha, too

With a side of therapy cards

A hybrid católica recuperando de las mentiras, como un buffet, tomo lo que me sirve a mí

I crave the ritual

Y con tu espíritu
Te paras y te sientas

Osana en las alturas,
bendito es el que viene en nombre del señor

The choir with the off key señoras, so comforting

Even now I sing at the top of my lungs at weddings y bautismos

And funerals too, between sobs

Entre tus manos, está mi vida señor, entre tus manos pongo mi existir
hay que morir para vivir

¿Cuántas veces has muerto para renacer? Completita y un poco cicatrizada
Pero con muchas ganas de existir

Dicen

Dicen que con un huevo por el cuerpo te sacas las penas
Las malas vibras
El mal de ojo

Con ir a la iglesia Con un tecito Con un panecito Con un abrazo

O tal vez un besito

"así, así" te dicen
Todos tienen el remedio Todos tienen un consejo

Con buenas intenciones, y a veces con malas también

Saturadas de información
Hasta las pestañas
Hasta el gorro

Hasta que ya basta!
Hasta que te cansas de preguntar y googolear

Apagas todos los aparatos Para pensar un poco

Con la velita
Con el tecito
Con el pan calientito

Con la música viejita y los recuerdos
las memorias de amor

Encontrando la paz
En esos momentos
Solo para ti

Sin necesidad de huir

Oleada

El mar y las olas
Me recuerdan del infinito

De mi insignificancia

Que mis problemas son como un grano de arena
que antes fui parte de una piedra grande

Que con el tiempo se disuelve
y no se distingue.

Warrior womyn

We carry broken hearts
but they are on the mend
Stitched together by a gentle hand
The needles made up of stories of strength
of pláticas infinitas
The yarn is colorful and sometimes only blue or red or pink or black

To stitch you back together

After all the losses and the wins
And in between times when things are good
They stitch messages of hope and love
the sewing kit is always ready for the next heartbreak.

Warrior womyn we celebrate together
Travel
Drink
Remember
Forget
Cry and
take selfies con el filtro bonito

Warrior womyn
They stitch their hearts back together
Sometimes they leave a stray, and it gets pulled away
But then you realize it was not meant to be there

Every stitch
Every color
Every story
These warrior womyn

They got their fine point needles
to rearrange and to mend.

When you watch someone die

Slowly over weeks in a hospital
you worry
You see their eyes glaze over and wonder if they feel the hurt and the love
You hope they see the love

When you watch someone die
You try not to complain as much
about having to pee all the time
you remember her swollen stomach
and the room was so cold as they stuck a needle in her to remove her pee
You don't complain as much about brushing your teeth late at night
when all you want to do is fall asleep
You don't complain about blow drying your hair, or taking a shower
'cuz all these things you take for granted
she wishes she could do
you are grateful you can control your bodily fluids

When you watch someone die that you thought would live forever
You feel lied to
Angry
Alone
Frightened
Worried

Yes, yes the stages of grief
You can shove it, don't need to hear it again

It's not so comforting

The drives to the hospital

The vigil around the bed

The smells

The freezing cold air

The lifeless body

You still worry that they are all alone in some hospital basement
Because it takes so long to get the coroner's report and all the dates at the cemetery and mortuary together

Some bodies never get claimed, 'cuz it's so expensive to die

You wish you were Jewish,
so you could sit with the body
You wish you were in the rancho,
where you could sit with the body
Then walk it over procession style in a wooden box to the church
then to the campo Santo
And get the whole process over with in a more humane way

Wish that everything wasn't for profit
At least not death

When you watch someone die
A little piece of your heart dies, too
But not for long
Because they come back to remind you
their love is true and infinite

My abuelita era pura magia

Era de las dignas
que no muestran mucha emoción

No somos de las que se tiran y chillán
Son las que se quedan calladas
Y se ponen a trabajar
Alimentar a todos

No son las que hacen escenas como en las novelas
Pero de vez en cuando si dan cachetadas y chanclazos

Nunca tuvieron el lujo de sentir nada
Porque la vida les enseñó a valerse por sí mismas y trabajar
Porque los hombres se van o se mueren

Todo se lo guardaban
Muy adentro
Las heridas muy profundas

De eso no se habla

A generation of stoic women
who suffered in silence
I wonder what you knew, what you felt.
Did you know that I could see your pain?
Did you know that you trapped the pain and the joy, too?
I feel you
I cry for you
Because even though the sadness was buried
It was always there

I have the therapy bills to prove it.

Entiendo abuela que me toca sanar
para que la tristeza no me hunda.

A mí
me toca vivir.

This is the price we pay

Today with my mommy in the clinical trials office
Depression
The way she looks down
Curves her spine and looks at the ground
Tears stream down her face
She's thought about it before
Ending her life
As I sit next to her remembering
The crying in the hallway
The hospitalization
The desperation in her voice
The pain she is in
Twiddling her thumbs
(I breathe deeply to avoid from sobbing)

It's her time to get help

She describes the gun, she almost used it
But she remembered her children

The gun, the gun, the gun, the gun

The memory loss
The list of meds
She's only 61
(I rub her shoulder in support)
This is the price we pay

The sadness
The unresolved trauma
The losses compounded
By the addicted son
The sick sister in Modesto
She gave it her all at the canneries and they gave her a pink slip and a heart problem
They said working with those metals all those years was perfectly safe,
I wonder if they would let their mother work there
This is the price we pay
The children of immigrants
Our parents' bodies wrung dry
Left to fight for decent health care
With a bag of medications in a zip lock bag

This poem might save you *(me)*

I want to write a poem,
a profoundly touching poem

that somehow makes several connections to things you're feeling, seeing, tasting
a poem that opens your eyes from a deep self-induced slumber
a poem that snaps you from your bed into Action Jackson
I want your mind to bend into shapes you never knew it could,
yoga style for the mind
a poem for the heartbroken, loveless, hopeless, soul who's lost their way 'cuz your path was laid out long before you were born, and you try your best to make your own, but it pulls you down as invisible and strong as gravity

I want my words to pull you out of quicksand and onto dry land that's no longer wet with your tears of regret and frustration,

I want to write a life-saving, self-soothing, truth speaking poem
that poem that rids your soul of fears and doubts,
a "limpia" poem, 'cuz the utopia ain't round the corner and neither are your dreams

I want to write an inspirational, sad, happy poem

that's filled with nostalgia for that time that never was

but your heart beats for it
It's there living in your memory

I want my poem to be that life jacket that pulls you onto shore

a collection of words that's never been written quite like this
that's so deep it touches down to your toes and sends electricity up your spine

truths a lie detector can't deny,
truth be told the poems been lying in my core under all the distractions,
words dusted off,
the poem of all poems,
to hug, slap, kiss you into your senses,

your private revolution brewing,
you hear, see, taste, smell, touch, breath, in out,

slowly grabbing hold of the magical wheel
'til it lands on *your number* kinda poem!

The thing about sisters

The sisterhood of the traveling chancla
Sisters know your story
They hold your hand and dry your tears when you're sad, or hold you down so you won't hit them, and
 they don't get mad when you lock the door to the room you share with your brother and slide notes under the door with scribbles saying this is you, ugly scribbles, 'cuz you think that will hurt their feelings
You jump on the bed together with a brush in hand and sing loud Daniela Romo songs
They don't mind you trying to listen in on the landline or read their diary or follow them like a puppy 'cuz they're so cool.
And you don't mind doing your fire marshall bill impression to make her friends laugh and sing on the phone to show off your untrained wannabe Mariah Carey, Whitney Houston voice
They play with you all over the house and backyard and even in church with the silly faces of sister language
They listen and ask your dad to buy Mcdonalds 'cuz you're the youngest and the cutest and dad will listen to you
You play hide and seek and listen to loveline and learn about STDs at the age of seven thanks to Ricki Rachtman and Dr. Drew

This Poem Might Save You *(Me)*

The soundtrack to your childhood, Chelo and Chalino, and Oldies and 90's R&B and KROQ too
They are just as terrified as you and help you find the lost shoe, book, crayon, cup, plate to help you not get in trouble and they harass the babysitter, Carmelita, to buy you something at the store on the way home from school.
They love you at your worst middle school awkwardness
You confess unspeakable truths in the bedroom and comfort each other always
They are your number one fan, and number two fan, or they compete for number one sometimes with your primas
all before the age of thirteen of course when the hormones make you crazy and makes you hate everyone
then you get into a groove when everyone is a grown up
except you're still the little sister or the middle sister or the big sister, you must defer to big sister always, 'cuz she knows best, 'cuz she had the worst parenting
you cry and laugh together and sometimes argue and get mad at each other and get hurt too
but sometimes you get to be the responsible one, too, you take turns and try to manage family trauma and drama together
you hold each other at funerals, and you play with each other's hair, and you all fluctuate and trade clothes from size 0 to size 16 through abortions and pregnancies, breakups, moves, travels, graduations, weddings, almost-divorces and babies, cute little fuzzy babies that look like… yo no se, I think all babies look the same, pero you love them instantly because they are an extension of you.
Hermanas, sisters, compañeras, silent co-conspirators, witnesses, advocates, holders of truth, selfless and stern when needed,
sisters are a gift from the universe,
from the deep connection of the soul.

Careless man

Scorched earth
      Crows gather
Darkened soil
      Smell of ashes

Yellow leaves drying out
dying
Brother tree
Sister tree
What have we done to you?

Coyotes, bunnies, squirrels, bobcats, gophers
Squeezed out
Burned out
by a careless man
Fire of destruction

Hungry, thirsty,
nature cries out
to deaf ears

As I stare at a half-empty water bottle
wondering why there's enough for those bottles in the fridge
but not for the trees
or the harvest

I murmur a silent prayer and say I'm sorry
I'm sorry we couldn't protect you
I hope some of you got away
Found safety

Escaped the fire started by a negligent man

I pray that the sky will bless us with a little rain
to soothe this scorched earth and restore some balance

to calm my aching heart as I stare at the damage

Untitled haiku #7

Red Sun Crescent moon
Dusk welcomes them both up high
In the sky this day

If only you see
The rhythms, the sways, the breeze
magic in the trees,

birds cawing, whistling
wings flapping gently, gliding
blue sky, turns to night

41 Lessons from 41 years on Planeta Tierra

1. Drink water.
2. Exercise makes me feel better, always.
3. Breathe a lot, slowly and through the nose.
4. Dancing and music conjures powerful magic.
5. Baby hugs cure all sadness.
6. A long talk on the phone with a friend soothes loneliness.
7. Therapy is good (it's ok to go many times).
8. So are self-help books.
9. Meditation helps too, even if it's only 10 minutes.
10. Sleeping 7 hours make me feel more human.
11. So do half hour naps (but more than half-hour makes me depressed).
12. Making the bed every morning makes me feel more at ease.
13. Worrying about things that haven't happened is exhausting.
14. Worrying about things that already happened is exhausting.
15. There's no need to rush, slowing down is hard but necessary.
16. Sometimes I'm a know it all and it's annoying.
17. Loneliness is my old friend, my constant companion.
18. But so is joy and laughter and smiles even if I'm faking it sometimes.
19. Friendships save lives.
20. It's ok to be alone.
21. Writing helps me process because storytelling is powerful.
22. Take risks even when it's terrifying, and wear hoops and red lipstick often 'cuz it helps.

23. We are all connected in our experiences, everyone has had to struggle in one way or another.
24. It is indeed a small world, so be cool fool 'cuz regret stings.
25. Racism sucks.
26. Everyone is just trying to live their lives; nobody cares that much about what you're doing (get rid of your imaginary audience).
27. I can feel safe, and it's ok to be scared, too.
28. Books can be your best friend; they are always there to transport you.
29. No need to save the new stuff for that someday, that day is today and it fits so just wear it already.
30. Cocktails are lovely, maximum 2, okay 3, or else shit gets ugly.
31. Remember the details of those beautiful days, later you will revisit them and they will bring you peace.
32. An Attitude of Gratitude is super annoying but also helpful.
33. Sometimes I choose the wrong partner (okay, a lot of times).
34. And it's okay, I always come to my senses, or my senses come to me in the form of a glaring issue that I can't ignore.
35. The ocean is just a drive away, and so worth it every time.
36. And so are all the vacations I save up for.
37. Be gentle with yourself.
38. Criticizing others is fun sometimes, but other times not so much. It can be cruel especially when I turn it on myself.
39. We are only here for a short time, and being an asshole doesn't help.
40. Be human first, after your coffee, of course.
41. Change is inevitable so get used to it, baby.

Airport blues

Wet bathing suits packed in
after a last splash in the pool and ocean
the beers and tequila swirling around in my tummy
Sometimes when I fly back from a trip, I feel lonely
It's the post-vacation blues, I know first world problems
Surrounded by people pero sola con mi soledad
Time to find the LAX shuttle and hop on
Head to union station, transfer to the gold line
(it takes forever) or take a lyft
Lyft driver is weird
Says some strange stuff, it's late so I just agree "uhum", and I'm tired
Finally, I get home to my dark apartment, to my solitude, no longer surrounded by people
But still loneliness lingers

Pink Suitcase

Torn a little
(Should I buy a new one?)
It's traveled with me to many destinations
Wheels dragging around
My precious possessions for a fabulous trip
Earrings and dresses with the tags still on in case you want to return it
Cremitas y perfumes, chargers a plenty
Pink suitcase suits me just fine
Don't need to spend a dime on another
Because it's worn marks remind me of where I've been, of my skin

Prayer for the pain

Las heridas siempre duelen
unos días más que otros
y se que has sufrido tú también
porque no es fácil escoger

un día el sol sale
pero sientes que no brilla para ti
aunque tengas que gritarlo,
no te lo guardes así
suelta el llanto,
suelta el dolor
por solo unos momentos
siente el calor de las almas alrededor

Las heridas siempre duelen
unos días más que otros
sana, sana, respira muy profundo

toma mi mano, y juntas nos desahogamos
¡Gritamos!
¡Qué no te consuma el dolor!
¡Qué no te consuma la adicción!
¡Qué no te consuma la desolación!

La vida es muy bella
aunque a veces también cruel
pero lo bonito es mejor
No te dejes caer….

una hija

solo pido que tengas una hija
no te quedes sola

dice mi mami.

No me ofendo, it's a compliment

Because the daughters, the three of us,
we do our best to help
To hug, to pay, to call, to drive, to pray, too.

The daughters save the family
The daughters work together

Una hija,
Solo una hija

Alguien que me cuide a mi si me toca llegar a la vejez.

Una hija.

It's Getting Hot in here/ So Hot in Here

these hot LA days most remind me of walking home from school
the sun burning us up
the heat rising from the cement and the lack of shade and the glaring sun in our faces

we ain't worried about SPF or wrinkles
and the tar from the playground they've been fixing forever, is stuck to my Prowings from Payless,
but they better last me 'til the end of the school year
the lingering smell of chemicals from the nearby factories in the air.

Walking home from school with my sisters
red in the face and stinky and stained with the free lunch and STARVING!
'Cuz them LAUSD lunches were gross.
Switching to Spanish for Carmelita, the babysitter,
And mad at Carmelita 'cuz she wouldn't buy me a Big Stick for a quarter
'cuz she has to send it to her family in México.

This Poem Might Save You *(Me)*

My braids all messed up, until we finnnnally get home, and the big bag
of oranges my dad buys from the men on the street are sitting there like a
sweet promise of relief from the heat,
so what if we ain't got no A/C
the plastic covered couches stick to my body,
so I sit on the floor in front of the TV, inches away, so what if mom says I'll
go blind.
It's more fun up close, anyway she's not home, I say to my smart aleck sister.

We sit in front of the TV peeling orange after orange with sticky fingers,
making our own montaña de cascaras,
our own mountain of orange peels we'll later fight about who has to clean
up,
while the Animaniacs theme music competes with Carmelita's novelas.

I forget about the big stick because the sweet oranges cooled me down,
and I'm not mad at Carmelita anymore,
'cuz she's a good babysitter and she's only 19
she came from my mom's pueblo to make some money and promised to
return, but she never did.
She stays, like the sun stays,
like the longing stays for a homeland that's also hot and sunny,
but over there, there are an abundance of trees and a river,
AND you can eat all the mangos and naranja/limas you want straight from
the tree.

Hospital Vending Machines

Grab the dollars and coins and walk down to the vending machine
When you need a break from the sickness

The processed food and neon lights in the basement provide a respite
The kids are restless anyway, you say

So, you grab your dollars and coins and walk down the hall
Past the sick, past the other families holding vigil for their own

To grab the overpriced chips or ice cream or water
Everyone with the same look of exhaustion and worry on their face

Or maybe you're just projecting

Baby boys hold your hand as you choose the right snacks to calm your heavy heart.

Inspired
       Inspiration
              Instinct
                     Intuition
                             Into a poem I am found.
                                       (and sometimes lost).

Dando vueltas

I met my dad at taco bell
Near where his condo used to be in Pacoima

I walked in and he was there

Sitting at a table
While the Ferris wheel of the upcoming fair shown bright
Large and looming in the background
Not open 'til the weekend
He said it would have been a good photo
A good ride to take together

Like the story I share with my father
The story of home

A ride we never took when I was a kid
Because time is funny that way, and divorces, too

This Poem Might Save You *(Me)*

Not always safe
Not always nice
But love is complicated that way

I sat in his girlfriend's condo
It was empty 'cuz she sold it and is moving out

She told me stories of travels with my dad
Asking him to corroborate

Strange feeling, not my mom, a lady so familiar with my dad
I peeked into the bedroom 'cuz the door was open and there were blankets set up on the floor for two

Strange feeling, he sleeps with her, too.
They are both retired and hoping to enjoy it with each other sometimes

As I said goodbye, she shared a joke, said my dad wouldn't wipe her butt when she's old, but she will wipe his

Hasta luego le dije, gracias por acompañar a mi papá en su vejez
It's comforting, strange, but comforting

Pues I had hoped it would be my parents together and I feel silly for feeling this way at 41
When I knew they didn't work out for many reasons, and they divorced when I was 20, old enough to know it was for the best, but still wish my parents could take care of each other in their old age
A fantasy, I know, because well maybe they'd be at each other's throats and fighting,

Pero me despedí de la señora that I met for the first time, my dad's compañera, and my dad hugged me tight and told me he loved me, I think it was a little uncomfortable for him too
'Cuz we old school that way

As I drove home the Ferris wheel shown bright with the possibilities of seeing it all from a bird's eye view, going round and round en la noche like my thoughts

Clean bathroom

As I wipe the mirror, I always get that moment
The woman in the mirror
Who is she?
Oh yeah, it's me
An adult cleaning her own bathroom, with the radio on loud and sweating
Not like the picture of Dorian Grey or the man in the mirror by MJ
It's me, Jesenia.

In my own apartment, where I pay my own rent, where I replace the light bulbs when they go out, even the one in the fridge that took me a couple weeks 'cuz I didn't want to go to home depot, and instead dealt with the minor inconvenience of looking inside a dark fridge

But I feel proud I found the bulb at CVS, and I didn't need much help, just the bulb in my bag to find the right one
as I squatted down to find it, a man looked at me strangely
perhaps I was talking to myself

I clean my space and I feel accomplished and search for adult stickers to get a reward for being self-sufficient
Instead, I buy lots of candles online

Where are the pictures of ladies like me?
Cleaning their own bathrooms and replacing their own light bulbs in apartments

They are there in the reflections if I look closely, in my own eyes

When the journal pages are complete

When the journal pages are
complete
The sadness creeps in
That funny feeling
All the feelings
 stories you tell yourself over and over
eternal heartbreaks and positive affirmations
annoying optimism you carry, 'til you don't
'Cuz sometimes it's hard to get out of bed.

Pages full of to-do lists and wishes and ideas to revisit later that you
sometimes don't
Random passwords
endings and beginnings
dreams and nightmares
laughter and tears echo through the pages
And quotes from the books you've read.

Doodles and swirls and your name over and over like in elementary school,
when writing your name was always soothing to your busy mind

Colorful ink
Neat letters when you are calm
Swirly handwriting you can't always understand when you are sad or mad
or anxious
Tear-stained ink
Journals piled up
No more blank pages

Til you pick up the next journal after a proper goodbye to the last.

Las movies

When I was a kid, we would go to the drive-in to see movies
My parents would tell us to hide in the back with a blanket so we didn't have to pay extra
Have to save money, of course

Then we started going to Commerce theater where they would steal your rims or car battery while you sat at the theater for 4 hours watching a double matinee with your family, my dad would silently whisper the translations to my momma, just like at home

One time we went to see Mrs. Doubtfire and I cried. Another time, we saw Pretty Woman with my elementary best friend Ana, and her parents weren't too happy about that, but hey, my parents didn't know it was inappropriate for kids. Those ratings meant nothing to them, so what if it was about a prostitute, it had a happy ending, right? Like all the protagonists from the novellas that get rescued by handsome men.

The Never-Ending story was a family favorite, my dad would change the words of the song and add our names,

And I loved it

We would go to Max Video in Maywood to get some movies, 3 for $10 for the weekend, for family fun time. We would sit around and watch them together
My parents didn't grow up going to the movies or renting them, the rancho didn't have those places
But there we sat watching movies en ingles together

Now I take my nieces and nephews to the movies, we sit and eat all the snacks we couldn't afford when I was a kid. I buy the popcorn, nachos, candy, soda, i-cee's y todo, I don't care how much it costs. We sometimes sneak in to watch a second movie for free, sometimes we bring in our lunch, subway sandwiches or tacos, food easy to eat in the dark

The movies were a way for us to hang out together, to watch TV as a family, to hear the whispered translations to my momma, a way to escape and enjoy for a very reasonable price.
I love the movies, renting them, seeing them at the movie theater, the smell of popcorn and processed foods, the complete darkness and then the lights come on and you step outside and feel a little disoriented pero feliz.

Sunday Service

I saw a bunny during the first 5 minutes of my hike
it ran up and stood still un buen presagio
it reminded me of resilience!
This bunny has many predators, coyotes and fires, humans, cats, and dogs,
yet there it was greeting me at 9am on the mountain top I love so much.

I walked in the heat and saw the usual folks with dogs and families, and hipsters, too.

I walked through the park and noticed a dropped white ford truck,
a clean slick truck, con nice rims y todo,
same one I had seen yesterday at the gas station,
owned by this veterano looking señor,
he was asleep in it, playing an oldie loud and with the windows open,
yesterday he had bought 2 forty-ounce beers.
Today he was napping at the park, maybe he's fighting with his hyna or vato

Then I walked to get my overpriced iced coffee and ran into my beautiful amiga on her way to get acupuncture.

Glanced across the street and saw the planned parenthood protestors
They pissed me off
Standing around praying, don't they have anything better to do?

Almost back to my apt, I see a black man with his bible, dressed in a suit,
walking into a Baptist church service,
the hall is used for hipster gigs
quinceañeras, y bodas, too

but today it was for church
the man was looking sharp and walking with purpose,
the service starts at 10:30am the sign said

I wondered if he was the preacher, or the preached to.
He walked gracefully, and greeted me good morning
Startling me, 'cuz sometimes I think I am invisible
I go so far inside myself that when strangers greet me, it takes me a minute to adjust
Good morning
bringing a smile to my face and his.

He seemed so sure of his faith and his Sunday service
I looked down at my workout clothes and decided it wouldn't be appropriate for me to join them

Though I crave the community and connection, too

The protestors, the coffee shop, the people in the park, me on my walk,
that's MY Sunday service
To observe, to enjoy, to listen to the sounds and stand with as much resolve as the planned parenthood protestors and as sure as the man walking into church

This is my Sunday service, my holy communion
Cafecito y pensamientos chiquititos
A hello and a good morning through a mask
A coincidence to see the same man
The neighborhood full of strangers all on our way to our own versions of Sunday rituals

Clown mask

Clown mask at the workshop
I chose to be analyzed
It was painful

My mask revealed
My jokes my shield

If I were an oldie, I'd be smile now cry later

The company I keep

I chose to dim my light for men
For the men I chose to love

I hid so much, I forgot where I went
Had to look at the map of my heart

Had to search with the lights on
Had to find my way back to me

But it was a treacherous journey
With booby traps a plenty
Attempting to sabotage me

Traps I laid out myself

Had to find my way back to me
Remove the traps, thirst traps and others

Had to remember to love all of me.

Planned parenthood protestors

They stand around outside harassing women who had to make hard decisions

Women like me
Women like me who at 19 walked in to get a termination
Would they have provided free childcare for me while I was at work or at school?
Would they pay my rent and bills when I didn't have enough?

They stand around praying and singing songs, but those things don't pay no rent
They don't pay those therapy bills, they don't make your shitty boyfriend a better person
They don't make you wanna raise babies you're not ready for

Planned parenthood protestors
Please pass on by
Go home and pray
Don't stay

15 Month Pandemic Home Transformed

Home is classroom (white board up so my bed doesn't show in the background)
Gym (with the YouTube videos and weights you borrowed and bought, too)
Therapy sessions (shut the windows so the neighbors don't hear)
Performance space for LIVE on the socials, even learned what Twitch was
Recording studio for podcast (make sure the neighbors are quiet, only the hum of the fridge)

Home (is the carefully crafted scene for the zoom background con libros y crocheted bernie and Selena Funko Pop, and Fridita black and white)
My studio apt (couch and bed and tables and chairs gifted to me).
My home (well, I rent but you get me)
My home
Became everything
Dancing en el tik tok,
Family reunions con audífonos
Transformed
Home, my refuge

Can I?

I can keep myself safe
I trust me
Little voice it scares me
Losing control
Just on the verge
Playing near the edge
Just how far can you go?

11:50 am highland park, CAlifaztlan, October 31, 2021

I forgot my phone
The horror
The fear
The pain

If it is not recorded, posted on IG or snapchat, or anywhere
Did it really happen?
Do the steps count, if they are not tracked and counted on an app?

If it is not photographed and hash tagged, and no one gave it a thumbs up
I ask you,
Did it really happen?

Tu Eres mi Tesoro

A child can make a toy out of anything
Just like my dad told us stories of how he grew up
Playing with rocks and sticks and whatever
Working hard, getting oranges and peanuts on January 6, día de los Reyes Magos, but no presents on Christmas
Reminding us of how lucky we are, (and this explains why he saves so much and doesn't want to spend on stuff he considers frivolous like eating out unless it's a buffet)
not having money or fancy toys does not stunt your imagination

Your inclination to play

I see that with my students, they remind me of my dad's stories

They play with EVERYTHING, much to my annoyance,
a piece of paper on the floor,
a sparkly sequin they found,
a broken zipper,
a piece of playdough on the bottom of the shoe
the found objects,
the real creators of authentic art,
of magic

tears, arguments, and fights have broken out over a stick or a leaf a kid found

and though it annoys me greatly, I appreciate it,
the joy of discovery, the limitless capacity to play
no matter how dark the world may be
no matter how hard their homes or community may be

the discarded paper becomes a smile, a folded creation
the lucky penny
the pigeon feather,
the broken wheels of a toy car
the piece of teddy bear stuffing
the spork
the water bottles flipping (the one I find the most annoying)
they sometimes offer me their little treasures
Like SEE this Miss, see the incredible beauty all around us
SEE how fun it is to play
SEE how to be resourceful
See how easy it can be to get excited about the world
All the treasures waiting to be discovered, if you just look

Sisters

My mom is the youngest of three sisters
The power of three
Like when genuflecting
persinándome
En, Nombre del Padre,
del Hijo,
y el espíritu santo

Is it blasphemous to say?
en nombre de la madre,
la hija,
y el espíritu divino femenino?

Tres hermanas luchando en California
Juntas apoyándose siempre
Conchita, Tía Chayo, y Tía Nina Panchita
Tia Panchita
La artista, la que todos quieren
Gone too soon,
Your silly humor chasing las muchachas con insectos
beautiful voice and delicious cooking

Tia Chayo
La luchadora
Que se vino primero
Para crear nuevos caminos y oportunidad
Enfermita pero siempre guerrera

Mi mami preciosa Conchita
La más Chiquita
La más atrevida
Defendiéndonos como fiera siempre
rezando, sonriendo, soñando

A trifecta of love
and strength,   and survival

The Falcon Knows More

Falcon on the streetlight by the freeway,
just chilling.
Taking a break
as the cars slowly crawl toward home.

Translation

I hate having to explain about the switch between inglés y español
The words exist and are born without limitations
Italics, footnotes, and asterisks*
Squiggly red lines BE GONE!

I have to translate for who?
Who can't understand as I switch between languages?

Language born from pueblitos en Chihuahua Mexico passed down from my parents,
To Maywood
To Bell
To Huntington Park
books read,
jobs and degrees acquired,
y todo in between

The feelings they show themselves and transcend language
Our cities, our streets, states are full of borrowed words,
California, Santa Barbara, San Diego
Tacos, burritos, aguacate

Occupied places, stolen words, twisted to conform to English

Los Yunited Estates
Es multi-cultural y multi-lingue
Tan diversos los acentos como las comidas

¿Por qué debo traducir?

En el dollar hay Latin
Quiero más libros, textos y cuentos, palabras que me reflejan

Tired of hearing
Too much Spanish
Too much spanglish
Too much English

The submission guidelines got me tied up
And tongue twisted
Spell check has got it all wrong

The words come out bilingue
Y con ESO me puedo expresar!

Group Text

Family group thanksgiving text
    how many turkeys?
While brother sits in jail
Two interventions in one week with him
Monday after work

Teaching kiddos having meltdowns
Paperwork and read alouds
    should we bail him out?
but he needs to go to rehab

    Thursday morning intervention
Shouting match commences between him and my older sis
Hotline calls
Brother sits
Nails dirty full of oil
Sun burned from being in the streets

Aunt lays dying in her bed
Long car ride with my mom
We sing, laugh, I squeeze her hand as she tells me her worries
      Should mom visit him in jail?
Public defender
           court ordered rehab we pray
Poetry readings
Birthday cake
Baby giggles
Hugs
Taking my nephew to the park
Dry my tears so he won't notice that I just spoke to his dad
struggle
All in one week
      joy and fears comingle in my heart
Grateful and scared at the same time
Working
      creating
smiling
      crying
maintaining
      (how do others do it?)
I put it away in a mason jar, in a locked box for later,
for when I can go through it

Glass Window Facts!

I accidentally brushed my teeth with **face cream, SPF 30.**
It was right next to the toothpaste

> (the cost of basic necessities in jail is way too high and disproportionally affects women of color [1])

I was preoccupied, thoughts of my little brother in jail. Went to visit him for the first time, I drove in past Magic Mountain,

> (I remember that one time we all went, screaming on colossus, with the ups and downs, never imagined he would be in a correctional facility down the street [2])

I drove along with the other folks driving home from a Thanksgiving holiday perhaps?
Provided proof of my vaccine and an ID,

> ("Across 34 state prison facilities, an average of 77% of prisoners are fully vaccinated, while only 63% of staff are fully vaccinated.")

saw all the other women there visiting too, some with little kids.
All with a look of resignation, fear, despair.
All there to board the bus to the prison to see their loved ones too,

All black and brown faces visiting

> (Black men are six times as likely to be incarcerated as white men and Latinos are 2.5 times as likely. [3])

And I saw ALL BLACK and BROWN faces behind bars

EXCEPT THE GUARDS of course, they were mostly WHITE [4]
> "Today, California's incarceration rates stand out internationally" [5]

Racing thoughts, worry, and fears
numbers too high, makes my head hurt and my heart cry
Do you know who profits from the prison system?
Did you know prisons have yelp pages? [6]

This Poem Might Save You *(Me)*

(North County Correctional facility has 19 reviews)
Did you know you can send Amazon packages?
and Nordstrom delivers there too?!

He should be in treatment, in-patient rehab, but he's not a rich guy who
can pay a fancy lawyer, get a slap on the wrist, and go to designer rehab [7]

So I accidentally brushed my teeth with cream,
I brewed my coffee with watered down water from the filter,
googled all the facts

Stressed myself out with worry and statistics

While baby brother sits in jail with all the others,

This is what systemic racism looks like,
what untreated addiction looks like in brown and black communities,

Too many little brothers, too many fathers, too many black and brown men locked up

While we sit and visit for only 30 minutes
(Not enough time, first 5 minutes I'm trying not to cry)

Visit for only 30 minutes

And hear our loved ones on the phone through a glass window

---

[1] Support SB555 https://www.youngwomenfree.org/take-action-support-sb-555-jail-facts-act/
[2] https://www.ppic.org/blog/uncertain-fate-awaits-prison-worker-vaccine-mandate/
[3] https://www.sentencingproject.org/criminal-justice-facts/
[4] 61.9% white, source https://www.bop.gov/about/statistics/statistics_staff_ethnicity_race.jsp
[5] Source https://www.prisonpolicy.org/profiles/CA.html
[6] https://www.yelp.com/biz/north-county-correctional-facility-castaic
[7] Just google any rich celebrity/rich guy with a drug problem/arrest and see

Baby Yoda, is that you Grandma?

Baby Yoda, Grogor or whatever he is called, reminds me of my grandma. I think it has happened to many, and I mean no disrespect to my grandma or grandmas everywhere.
You see the wrinkled face, the big eyes, the quietness of the creature, and the love felt so familiar.

The unconditional love, the contrasts of worlds and words

Grandma came here, never spoke English, took care of all the grandkids, traveled up and down on the 5 freeway to be with my tía in Modesto, never drove a car and always walked, her cane and walker and wheelchair only came later, when she was in her 90s.

the Mandalorian reminds me of my grandma
worlds colliding
tenderness and violence
beautiful wrinkles and soft skin

This Poem Might Save You *(Me)*

so I sat and watched it for hours
seeing my grandma in this tiny green creature
crying and crying at the sight, and I immediately bought a doll that I want to carry everywhere,
that I want to hug a lot too, because it reminds me of her so much.

The love that it stays but it breaks your heart.

In her final years, I saw her become more fragile and quieter too,

I wish we would have understood her more, had the Jedi powers to read her mind, and feel her thoughts.

I helped her use the bathroom one time when we went to Santa Paula for a family party. I was so scared to hurt her, the bruises on her arms showing the many falls she had already had. I held her and she peed and then I helped her onto the bed with too many mattresses like princess and the pea.

You abuelita, were so tired already, but you stuck around as long as you could until your quality of life was so diminished, it could hardly be called living.

I searched for pictures on my laptop and found too few. I searched and searched to find more memories of you.

I search for you sometimes. I forget you are gone.

I search for your face and maybe that's why I saw it on the Mandalorian, because I needed a reminder of you, of your love and quiet strength and wisdom too,
because sometimes the loneliness is too much,
the worry running circles in my head, scaring me and I search for you.
I searched for that lifeline, and I found it in Baby Yoda's face, silly as it sounds. You showed up in a funny place for me to cry and laugh at the comparison.

Christmas Day

Some families go to jail to visit loved ones on Christmas day
Some families are mourning the loss of a loved one
                         To cancer, to age, to an absent parent, to a broken
                                                                 heart
some families drive to prison on Christmas day to visit their son, and only one person can go in go in for their 30-minute visit that took 2 hours, to drive, to plan to schedule

mother and father wait, father has to stay behind, "thanks for ruining Christmas" he says to the guard as he walks head down back to his car

some girlfriends and wives go to prison on Christmas day to visit only to be told that there is a lockdown, and she can only sigh and say it's the second time she has driven out to see him and can't go inside

some families sit worried on Christmas day about the rent due on January 1st, is there rent drive they can sign up for?

Some families miss their fathers, uncles, brothers, sisters, husbands, mothers, abuelas

Sometimes because they are stuck in immigration detention centers
Far away
Whatsapp and letters are not enough, not on Christmas day

Some families drive in the rain with bundled up little kids and prayers for a 30 minute visit

joy and pain
They comingle
The delight of many tamales, fury of wrapping paper, hugs, songs at midnight

On Christmas day I reflect, I rest, I embrace all the families with an open heart
In prayer for those families grieving
Grieving all year, in this system of injustice
But magnified on Christmas day
The holiday cheer, stifling,
    The holiday cheer, heartwarming too
        singing Christmas carols at the top of my lungs, driving home
Seeing the tears on the faces of the women walking out of their jail visits, on my mommy's face too.
Celebration of Christmas day
    The opposites collide

the santa hat, baby jesus in the manger, aretitos de arbolitos navideños, Christmas lights and tinsel, light the candles to pray on this Christmas day

Baby Mario

Spins
in   circles

round   and   round

shrieks with delight

throws toys and says Uh-Oh

                (like the Uh-Oh bear sis got for Christmas but she wanted
                      Teddy Ruxpin, now she has a real life boy!)

He points and says ducks a lot
                          (there are some ducks nearby)
              (oh and also the song 5 little ducks is well received)

He smiles and cries and holds his breath too

His little teeth multiplying by the minute
                                  (or so it seems)

Baby Mario spins in circles

Runs and waddles and shakes his head no when I ask him if he needs a diaper change
(his mommy and daddy do it best, convenient excuse for me)

Baby Mario is a fierce, chubby bundle of joy
                                                          (most of the time)

A combination of sarcasm and generally under-whelmed,
                  occasionally asking for Bum (little baby bum song)
                                          or um (food)
signing please and thank you and leche and all done

love to watch him explore
pick up rocks and grunt and ROAR!

Baby Mario spins in circles,
what a blessing,
a heart expanding 15-month life form
Nurtured and protected born in a strange COVID time,
mommy and daddy all alone in a hospital room,
they made a little warrior
Fed and bathed and combed and posed
Onesies, toys, bottles, blankies and more
What a miracle to behold!

Wilted

The garden is dead

Though it lives on in your feed

Surrounded by likes

Tree

>We planted a tree
>
>On someone else's property
>
>Is it thriving?
>
>Or did it topple with the powerful storms?
>
>Was the foundation weak?
>
>Did it make it to 2022?
>
>I don't know, and I won't go look.
>
>No shade to the tree,
>
>Grow on!
>even though our love did not.

I forget you

I forget you
At first I count the hours
Then the days
Then the weeks
Then the months

Til they add up to forgetting the hurt

My heart on the mend

I am not a mom and why do you care?

I am a human female woman

I am 41

I am sometimes working on myself and other times not so much

I am not a mom and that is not your problem

Though sometimes you make it so

Shame and blame and questioning looks

I hate that it affects me
I hate that it makes me doubt myself
Makes me wonder if I am indeed broken

I am not a mom,

I AM a human female woman
Perhaps my anatomy, my womb could grow a life, but why should it have to?

Don't have to explain myself to you
I am not a mom and that is not your concern

YET I wrote a whole ass poem

Tears for Fears: The Poem, Not the Band

Free-flowing tears
lead to words.
Water transformed into fears released!

Fuera miedo!
Fuera tristeza!

Our collective tears could end the California drought!

Tears for loss,
for anger,
for love,
for delight,
for it all.

So cry on, my sister!
       Release! Cleanse! And REPEAT as needed.

Agua,
aguita linda
que me limpia.

                                                    Water
                                         Precious water
                                           You cleanse me

Ode to my Ears

        Thank you for holding my glasses in their place,
my mask
my cute earrings
        they make my outfit POP!

Ears thank you for helping me LISTEN and HEAR

Hear the Helicopter swirls and LA traffic, hum of electricity

The powering down when the lights go OUT

The neighbors' keys in the door
The walking up the steps

The dogs barking in the distance

Raindrops on my AC

Birds
laughter
random screams from my nephews when I'm on the phone with my sisters

the giggles and the tears

the upstairs neighbor stomping her feet
the thrilling sound of packages dropped at my door,
the mail man and his multiple keys jingling to deliver those holiday cards

thank you ears for the
music,
the whispers,
the memories
the richness of sound,

Listening to the love all around me

the perfect symphony conducted by the five senses
combining to experience
the mundane,
the heartbreak
and the magnificent

Schools are magical spaces

"What have you learned in school," I ask?
How to be a friend,
to be kind,
to do calm breathing,
empathy,
how to write my name, and my friend's name too.

Some things can't be measured in a test.

How do you measure a smile?

Schools are magical spaces.
We thrive under the worst conditions,
but it comes with a toll.
Massive droves quitting,
mental health days not a luxury we can afford.

We learn each day

in SPITE of the lack of resources.

We learn!

Even under the crushing weight of all the needs,
We learn!
We adapt and survive,
so tired of the bureaucracy and red tape,
all the talk,
tired of teacher appreciation day.
Can't we just get treated with more respect?
Can't we just be treated as professionals?
Can't we just have the toys, the TAs, and books we need?
Can't we have less standardized soul-crushing tests
without having to beg and threaten to strike every year?
Can't I get my teeth checked without a massive bill?

We don't get those corporate perks.
The taxes get taken out of MY check,
while businessmen get tax write-offs,
find tax loops,
get bailed out.
WE have forever student loan debt.

Schools ARE magical spaces,
but we deserve MUCH, MUCH, MORE!

Weekly Screen Time Report, Who Asked You, Bro?

5 hours and 44 minutes,
Down 22%.
Weekly screen time report,
you averaged 4 hours and 21 minutes a day.

Every Sunday I am racked with guilt.
It's the Catholic in me,
I won't disable the report.

6.1-inch display
holds so much of my attention,
distracts and confuses me.

I want lips like Judy in the Jetsons had.
The floating red lips were her best friend.

This Poem Might Save You *(Me)*

Didn't want nosy Alexa or Siri who doesn't understand my Chicana English.

The floating red lips were fun.

Not like the ads, and the likes, and the tik tok pendejadas.
How many people watched the video of the dude dancing?
It blows my mind.

5 hours and 31 minutes,
oh, ok.
What did I do?
Watched other people living their best lives,
their loves,
potential vacation spots.

Outfits, babies, cars,
virtual pin boards,
experiences to be tagged.

What could I have done those five hours a day?
So many books read
And muscles made.

How many missed human interactions?

My full attention on one thing?
    Maybe.
If my phone is smart, am I dumb?
How many smiles and conversations missed?
How about good ole boredom?
Does that exist anymore?

I dread the weekly screen time report.

Shall I change my behavior?

Probably No.

El Arroyo

I bathed, swam, jumped in the same waters my mom did as a child.
En el arroyo de Dolores, Chihuahua,
Those same waters.

Water holds memories,
And I remember.

Our hikes there, to splash around, our stuff in bags, un jabón, a snack,
Chanclas on.,

Water holds memories, and I remember.

I remember we would splash around in our T-shirts and shorts, no bikinis muchacha.
Jump into the cold river water,
Refreshing after a long walk there.,

El arroyo where my grandma, mom, and tías once swam together too.

Water
El arroyo
Climbing trees,
Lavando ropa

Throwing rocks at peering boys

No Llorona here that drowned her children

Only women splashing and laughing

Women dreaming
Women hoping
Women loving

Water holds memories, and I remember

The ways our bodies moved
Weightless
Forgetting LA and the bills and the factories

And don't forget to dunk your head

We were baptized and renewed in those waters.

Acknowledgments:

My heart is full of gratitude for Davina Ferreira and the Alegría Magazine and Publishing family. The Wednesday Writing Workshops gave me the life and support I needed to embrace writing and make time for creativity.

Much appreciation to my UCLA Writer's Workshop pandemic writing group with Faye Peitzman and the wonderful community of educators who showed up on Zoom. A special thanks to Melissa Berlant, who made it possible for us to be together through these strange times.

To my colleagues at UCLA Community School who make miracles happen every day! To my brilliant, funny, and loving students and their amazing families who inspire me. *Gracias por dejarme ser su maestra y por enseñarme tanto todos los días.*

I am grateful for all the opportunities to share my work. To Fernando Funes and Elvia Susana Rubalcava. SIMS library of poetry. Yellow Arrow Publishing. Sarah R. Chavez from OndaLive. Lalo Alcaraz at www.pocho.com, and Mujeres de Maiz.

I thank my lovely friends who support me and cheer me on every day –too many to name but know that you are in my *corazón!* To the amazing people at CASA 0101: Josefina Lopez and Margaret Medina, for creating spaces that encourage our communities to create.

To my chosen family of *mujeres chingonas:* Beda, Chita, Lucy, y Liliana. Thank you for the vacations, meals, good ole fashion cries, for hearing me talk about this for so long, and always saying *que sí se puede!* My *amigo* y podcast partner, Jaime Mayorquin, thank you for always encouraging me to write and write some more.

To my *familia chula, mis hermanas* Lucero and Erika. You uplift me, make me feel loved, and accept me as I am. Lucero for always reading my first drafts, supporting me, and taking my calls. My *primas* who are also like sisters: Veronica, Ambar, y Carmen. My brothers David and Robert, I love you and am always rooting for you. My amazing nieces and nephews, who are so much joy –thank you for making me the cool *tia!* The future is yours!

To my lovely parents and the state of Chihuahua. The long trek my dad made to the United States. Your courage and your hard work are much appreciated. Love you pa!
Mami Preciosa Conchita, la quiero mucho. Gracias por llevarnos a su ranchito, y gracias por dejarme soñar. Por ser tan linda, por reírse conmigo, por todo su sacrificio y amor.

A mis angelitos en el cielo, Tia Panchita y Abuela Josefina. Siento que siempre están conmigo. Me urgen que escriba y que recuerde.

I thank the trees and the beautiful creatures that greeted me on my hikes: the coyotes, hawks, bunnies, turtles, and crows.
Thank you to my beautiful and complicated city of Los Angeles.

Sobre todo, gracias al universo inmenso que siempre me da lo que necesito.

This Poem Might Save You *(Me)*

Photograph by Teresa Zavala

Bio:

Jesenia Chavez is a proud Chicanita, public school teacher, writer, poet, and storyteller. She is a border-crossing, Spanglish-speaking, *bachata*-dancing, ukulele-playing human trying to make you laugh, cry, and giggle at the absurdities and beauty in the world. She has kept a diary since elementary school, which is filled with witty observations of the life of a Mexican girl in Southeast Los Angeles (or as the young kids say, #SELA) who keeps losing her *chanclas*. Her writing is inspired by her parents' migration from Chihuahua, Mexico, to Los Angeles, California, and the trips back and forth.

Jesenia attended the University of California, Santa Barbara, and majored in Chicano studies and sociology with a minor in history. There, she solidified her love of performance and theater by participating in the Chicano theater group, Teatro Nopal. She found her poetic voice in Dr. Chela Sandoval's class and through her work in the multicultural center, where she first saw performers of color making a living as artists. Jesenia then pursued her teaching credential and a master's degree in education from the University of California, Los Angeles. #latinawithamasters #cancelstudentloandebt

Her teaching career as a sixteen-year veteran of the Los Angeles Unified School District provides her with a passion for social justice because our chronically underfunded and underserved communities deserve more.

#fullyfundourschools. In her first few years of teaching Jesenia was laid off, rehired, and transferred. She went on strike in the rain. #redfored. She has also taught kindergarten and first grade in both English and Spanish during the pandemic. #resilient

Her writing reflects the sense of loss in the rapidly changing landscape of Los Angeles, and the stark inequalities one can observe on any given street. She relishes the small moments when she can catch her breath and put pen to paper. Jesenia also co-hosts *Qué Me Cuentas (What Can You Tell Me)*, a storytelling podcast featuring diverse experiences in the Latinx community. She believes in the healing powers of storytelling, poetry, dancing, nature, and hugs. Find her on Instagram at @chabemucho, @quemecuentaspod, or drinking fancy coffee at your local café.

Email: jesenia.chavez80@gmail.com

www.ingramcontent.com/pod-product-compliance
Lightning Source LLC
Chambersburg PA
CBHW070047120526
44589CB00035B/2360